To Our Children's Children
Journal of Family Memories

To Our CHILDREN'S CHILDREN

Journal of Family Memories

Bob Greene

AND

D. G. Fulford

Main Street Books
Doubleday
New York London Toronto Sydney Auckland

A MAIN STREET BOOK
PUBLISHED BY DOUBLEDAY
a division of Bantam Doubleday Dell Publishing Group, Inc.
1540 Broadway, New York, New York 10036

MAIN STREET BOOKS, DOUBLEDAY, and the portrayal of a building with a tree
are trademarks of Doubleday, a division of
Bantam Doubleday Dell Publishing Group, Inc.

ISBN 0-385-49064-X

IRSTLY

*Y*OU COLLECT a lot of memories over a lifetime. Here's a place to keep some of them.

Hundreds of thousands of families have enjoyed telling their stories through the pleasurable act of remembering, using the precise, evocative questions in *To Our Children's Children: Preserving Family Histories for Generations to Come*. The one request we hear time and again, however, is for a book with room to write the answers down.

To Our Children's Children Journal of Family Memories is just that: a selection of questions from *To Our Children's Children* that make recording a personal history as easy as writing a letter. When you have finished with this journal, it can become a lasting part of your family's life—something to cherish forever.

The important thing to remember about writing a family history is that there is no right way or wrong way to do it. These questions are meant as suggestions, as a guide. You do not need to answer every question in the journal to have a beautiful family history. Not every question will appeal to every person. Choose the ones that you want to answer. If a question about your grandchildren reminds you of a story about yourself as a child, then get that childhood story down on the page. This is your book—by recalling your stories, you'll get a chance to reflect on your life and paint a picture of your times. This can be the greatest gift you can ever give to your family—now and for generations to come.

That's what this journal is—a place to put your stories. One place to keep them together, safe and lasting.

Family stories are treasures made of words. Entrust them to these pages and hold them in your hand, then pass them along.

This journal is dedicated to

Our Grandchildren

What is your name? What state were you born in? What city? What
hospital? How old are you? What is your birthdate? What is your spouse's
name? What is your anniversary date? How many children do you have?
How many grandchildren? What are their names? How old are they?

My name is Laurel MacDougall Cronin. I was born at Newton Wellesley Hospital in Newton, Mass, on Jan. 15, 1942. I married Corky Cronin on June 22, 1963. We have 3 wonderful children, 2 grandson & one little angel girl on the way. Her Mommy is Kelley and the boys Mommy is Meaghan. Their Uncle is Jed

What is, or was, your occupation? Who is your next of kin? What is your religion? Do you live in an apartment, a house, a condo, or a retirement home? What is your nickname? What was your mother's name? Your father's name? Your grandmothers' names? Your grandfathers' names? What did you call them?

Were your parents and grandparents born in America? If not, where were they born? What circumstances brought them to the place where you were born? Were there people already there whom they knew, or did they come into the community alone? Was the community welcoming to them?

Do you have brothers and sisters? What are their names? How old were you when they were born? Do you remember the first time you saw them? Do you remember ever playing a trick on your brother or sister? What pictures come to mind when you think about playing together?

What about your aunts and uncles? What did they look like? Did they play an important part in your growing up? Did you play with your cousins? Did the family get together much casually, or did you have to travel and dress up to spend time together?

Did your grandparents' house have a special cooking smell? What did their couch feel like? Do you remember any special stories your grandmother or grandfather told you? Did you sit on a lap when you heard these stories, or did you hear them when you and your grandparent were walking hand-in-hand? Do you tell any of these stories to your own grandchildren?

Was yours a religious family? Did you all attend services together? What did your father do for a living? Your mother? Your grandparents?

Who were you named for? If it was a relative, did that make you feel especially close to that person, or did it put undue pressure on you?

Did your family say grace? Did you sit down at the table together for every meal? Was it at the same time every day? Who sat where? What was the dinner table configuration?

Do you have a piece of furniture or family heirloom that belonged to your parents or grandparents? What is it? Does it have a place of honor in your home?

When you think back on your mother and father now, what do you realize
about their lives that you didn't understand when you were growing up?

Did your father have a favorite saying you can remember him repeating? How about your mother? Do you sometimes find their words coming out of your mouth? Did your family pass down any superstitions?

What did the home of your growing up look like? Was it a house or apartment? What color was it? Was it stone or wood? One story or two? Can you remember the view out of any of your windows? What did you look out on? Your neighbors' houses? A row of stores? What stores? Or fields, woods, water, or mountains?

Who delivered to your house? A milkman? An iceman? A laundry man? An egg man? Or did you shop with your mother? At what kind of stores? Was there much music in your house? Did you listen to a radio or Victrola? Do you remember it being a quiet house or one filled with noise?

Were there books in evidence around your house? Was there a special room in the house considered the library? Which of your parents' books do you remember reading? Which books do you remember them reading?

What was the street like where you lived? Busy or quiet? Brick or paved? Was there a stoplight or stop sign on the corner? Can you remember your parents adding something they'd always wanted to the household of your growing up? A washing machine, maybe? A new icebox? An extra car?

Who was your best friend in the neighborhood as a child? Did you play at your homes or mostly in the streets and playgrounds and fields? What do you remember about your friend's house? About your friend's family? Did you have a secret path you used to take to go meet your friend?

Did you collect anything growing up? Bugs, baseball cards, marbles, china figurines? Did you have pets? What were their names? Do you remember when they came to live with you? Do you remember how they died?

Did you have chores around your house? Did you have to mow the lawn? Rake the leaves? Did you baby-sit for neighborhood children? Did anything unusual happen while you were baby-sitting?

How did you go downtown and get back home? Car, trolley, walk, horseback? Can you remember your first trip downtown? How was your neighborhood lit? Streetlights, porch lights? Describe your neighborhood. Was it rural or suburban? Was it green or concrete? Did anyone in your neighborhood have a fancy garden? A horse? A gazebo? A tree you liked to climb?

Where did you go swimming? What were your favorite board games? What was the name of your favorite doll or stuffed animal? Did you have an imaginary friend when you were growing up? Were your parents aware of your imaginary life? Did they play along?

Do you remember your favorite bedtime story or poem? What one do you remember your parents reading to you? Which do you remember reading to yourself? Were you afraid of the monster under the bed? What did your parents do to stop those fears?

Did you attend religious school? Did anyone from your neighborhood go, too?
Did you go to camp? Do you remember any counselors or the names of any of
your teams or activity groups? Were you homesick?

What were the neighborhood landmarks where you grew up? The ice cream shop? Drugstore? Barbershop? Grocery store? Flower shop? Shoe repair shop? What do you remember most vividly about them? What did your neighborhood sound like at night? What did it look like first thing on a summer morning?

What was the name of your elementary school? How big was it? Was it a public or a private school? Was it in a residential neighborhood with lots of trees around it or on an urban street? What did the school building look like? One story or two stories? Brick, wood, or stone?

Did you ride a bus to school? Do you remember anything that happened on that bus? Or did you walk? By yourself or with your brothers and sisters or a group of kids from the neighborhood? Do you remember sitting at long tables or individual desks? Do you remember sitting next to anyone in particular?

What was the playground like at your school? Was there a swing set? Tetherball? What games did you play on the playground? Did you ever play with the older kids, or did you stick with your own age group? Do you remember "getting" a concept? Cursive writing, maybe? Do you remember the moment when you first learned to read? Was schoolwork hard or easy for you?

Did you used to get excited thinking what you were going to wear on the first day of school? Did you ever go to a school where you had to wear a uniform? What was your attitude about school? Were you interested in it or bored by the whole thing? Was there ever a time that you were secretly sad that it was vacation time, or did you feel the joy in days off even then?

Did you eat lunch at school? Did you bring it, or was there a cafeteria? What did your lunchbox look like? Do you remember any field trips your class took? If you lived in the city, did you go to a farm? Did you visit a factory?

Did you ever win any awards at school? Were you in a scout troop? Who was the leader? Where did you meet? Did you have class plays or room programs? Did you have big parts in them or were you stage shy? Did you ever have to sing a solo? What costumes did you wear?

Do you have any friends who went with you all the way from elementary school through high school? Were you ever the new kid at school?

Can you remember a historic event that happened when you were in school?

Who told you about it? Your teacher? Your mother when you got home?

What did you do in the summertime when there was no school?

Do you like your birthday or do you dread it? What birthday do you remember the most from your youth? What kind of parties did your parents give you? Was your cake made at home, or was it store-bought? Did anyone ever give you a surprise party? Were you surprised?

Is there a Christmas present, a Hanukkah present, or a birthday present that sticks out in your mind? Who gave it to you? Was it a surprise or something you'd been wanting and wanting?

What was Halloween like for you growing up? Did you play tricks on people? What costumes do you remember wearing? What children did you go trick-or-treating with? What Halloween candy do you pass out now?

Did you ever get flowers for Valentine's Day? Did you every get candy in a heart-shaped box? Do you send valentines now? Do you still get them? Do you like to go out on New Year's Eve? What was the fanciest New Year's Eve party you ever attended? Do you make New Year's resolutions? Do you have a "good luck" dish that you eat on New Year's Day?

When was the first Father's Day you felt like a father? The first Mother's
Day you felt like a mother? What did your children do for you in celebration?
What did you do for your parents on those days? Where did you go for
Thanksgiving? Was there a dish your family was assigned to bring? Was
there a centerpiece that your family used every year? How about now?

Did you go on picnics growing up? What did you eat? Where did you go?
Do you remember a holiday you had to spend alone?

What was the name of your high school? What kind of neighborhood was it in? What street was it on? How many students went there? What did the hallways look and feel and sound like? What was your high school mascot? What were your school colors? Do you remember any of the cheers?

What teachers do you remember? Why? Did he or she ever make a comment about your work that stuck in your memory? What kind of extracurricular activities did you take part in? Were you on the school paper? A sports team? Were you a class officer? A cheerleader? Were your friends involved in the same activities you were? What was your favorite song in high school?

Did you study a foreign language? Have any phrases from that class stuck with you? Were you ever able to use that language on a vacation or in your community?

Who did you go to your prom with? What did you wear? What was the theme? Did you dance much? Did you give, or receive, a corsage? Did you have a class ring? Was it a big expense for you to buy it? Did you ever trade rings with anyone? Did you go steady?

Were you a rebel? Did you hide anything from your parents? Did you ever skip school? Were you ever caught? Did you ever get disciplined at school? What was your infraction? Were you really in the wrong?

Did you have a hobby, or did you spend your high school years mostly just hanging around with your crowd? Did you have any part-time jobs? What did you do in the summer? On weekends? Where did your crowd hang out? Did you go to a diner or a drugstore or a grocery or the library or a neighborhood gas station? Did you usually go right home after school?

What were the clothing trends when you were in high school? Did you follow those trends? What did your parents think? Did they like the way you got yourself up, or were your looks distressing to them?

Was there a library at your school? Did you utilize it or have fun with your friends there? Can you remember a particular book you checked out? Was it for your reading pleasure or for a report you were working on? Did you ever hang out with anybody from a completely different group? Did you have any friends from different schools?

Did science or math come hard to you? Did art or English come easy? Where did you sit to do your homework? In your room or at the kitchen table? Were your brothers and sisters with you, or did you work alone? Did you have the radio playing?

What did you discover about yourself in high school? Did you learn a skill that you could take out in the world with you? Were you sad when it ended, or were you ready to leave it all behind?

Have you ever attended a high school reunion? What truths did you learn about your class while you were there? What truths about your community that you might not have thought about before? If you, today, could have one conversation with yourself when you were a high school student, what would you say?

If you went to college, where did you go? Why did you choose that school? Did you have friends who went there, or was it the locale? How much was tuition? Was it difficult to afford? Did you receive financial assistance or a scholarship? A loan? Was your school large or small? What was it known for? Where else did you apply? Did you attend any kind of graduate school?

What was your living situation? Did you live in a dorm or a room off campus? Who was your roommate? Did you get along? How did you decorate your place? Were you comfortable there? Did you join a sorority or fraternity? What was rush week like?

When you first got to college, were you thrilled to be away from home? If you were homesick, what did you do about it? Write letters? Cry? Confide in someone? Or try to hide your feelings? If you were thrilled to be at college, were you quick in making friends? Who was your first friend there? Did you remain close through the years?

What was your major? Why did you pick it? Were you ever able to use anything you learned in college in your profession? In your life? Was there a professor who made a special impression on you? Were you able to take more than one class from this person?

Were there big party weekends at your college? Did you attend these functions? Were you able to get home for the holidays? How did you get there? By train? By bus? How long did the trip take? Did you meet anyone you remember on one of these trips? Did anything memorable happen?

Did any famous performers or lecturers appear at your college? Were you involved in campus politics? Did you have a part-time job when you were in school? Did you pull all-nighters studying?

What did you notice about students from other parts of the country? Accents?
Different taste in clothing? Did you change much at college? Did your parents
notice? Did your friends back home notice? Did they mention it to you?

What degree did you get? Did you attend graduation? Did you win any accolades at college? Phi Beta Kappa? Valedictorian? Magna cum laude? Do you think you made the most of your college years, or would it have been more advantageous for you to have gone later on?

Were you in the military? What were your rank and serial number? Were you drafted, or did you enlist? What was the first you saw of the service—the enlistment center? What did you see there that made you want to sign up? What was it like at the draft board?

What was the name of your company? Did it have a nickname? Did it have a mascot? Where were you stationed? Where did you go through basic training? How tough was it? How quickly did you move up through the ranks? Who was the first officer you admired?

Did you win any medals or citations? What for? Where do you keep that medal now? Is it prominently displayed in your house, or is it stashed away in a drawer? Who handed it to you? Was there a ceremony? What did your uniform look like? How did you feel you looked in it? Do you still have any of it in a closet somewhere?

When you think of your years in the service, what landscape describes it best? Flat, low ground? Mountains? A long, steep highway? What USO entertainers did you see perform? Which of your buddies did you sit with when you saw the program?

When did you first see combat? Did it take you by surprise, or did you know it was coming? When did you first see death? Did you lose any of your good friends? When you get together with your buddies to tell war stories, what stories do you tell?

Do you remember your homecoming with your parents? What did you have to eat for your first meal back home? Was there a love waiting for you? Did the war make you ready to settle down, or did you come home in a more celebratory mood? How difficult was the transition from the military back to civilian life?

Were you married to a serviceman or servicewoman, or did you have a
sweetheart in the service? Do you remember when they got their orders? How
did you react outwardly? Inwardly? Was a separation like that a common
occurrence for your friends during the war years?

How often did you write? Did you write at the desk in the living room or lying on your bed? How did you sign your letters? Did you write to any servicemen or servicewomen other than your sweetheart? Did you ever hear news of the war on the radio or television that affected your loved one directly? Did you find you were frightened every time the news came on? When did you usually listen?

What was your favorite radio show growing up? What did your radio look like? What room was it in? Did your family sit around and listen to programs together? Did you ever go see a favorite performer in concert when you were young? Frank Sinatra? Tommy Dorsey? Elvis Presley? What is your preference in music? Are you a country fan, rock and roll fan, or do you listen to classical music exclusively?

When did you get your first TV? Did you buy it so your family could view a special show or event? What room did you put it in? How much did it cost? Who actually carried it into your house? Was your family one of the first in your neighborhood to have a TV? How much TV do you watch? Do you watch more now than you used to? Which show have you continued to enjoy over the years? Do you ever watch soap operas?

What was the last movie you saw? What was the first movie you saw? What movie have you wanted to see more than once? What is your favorite Walt Disney film?

Do you attend sporting events or any events in an outdoor arena in your town? Rodeo? Car races? Football games? How important is reading to you? Do you have an author whom you follow? Have you ever been a member of a reading club? How about a book mail-order club? Do you usually go for the selection of the month?

Which comedian makes you laugh the hardest? Do you like them squeaky-clean or do you go in for racier types? Did you ever buy comedy albums? The Button-Down Mind of Bob Newhart *or something like that? Did you listen in a family group?*

Do you and your spouse enjoy the same entertainers and same types of entertainment? Or does each of you have a different set of friends with whom you attend performances? Who is your favorite talk-show host? What was the most fascinating program he or she had on? What is it about the host you like? Have you ever been in a television studio audience or called a talk-radio host and had your voice go on the air?

What TV performers have you seen come and go? Johnny Carson? Ernie Kovacs? Red Skelton? Do you miss their shows, or are the newer ones fine with you? Where were you during "Howdy Doody Time"? Were you in the kitchen fixing dinner? Were you in the car coming home? Were you lying on the floor in front of the set?

What poetry do you find accessible? What lines from poems stick in your mind?

What was your first job? Your first real job? Did you start out in an after-school job that had any relation to what you ended up doing? Were you as nervous on the first day of your real job as you were on the first day of your after-school job?

Has anyone helped you up the ladder, even with the first job? Was it easy for you to ask for or accept this help? Are you union or management? Do you feel as if you were in the right business for you? What would have been your dream career?

Were you friendly with your coworkers? Is there one you particularly remember? Did you ever socialize in their homes, or did you sit at a table with them at a company picnic? Did you go out to lunch together? Did you call them at night or on the weekends just to talk?

What was your boss like? Was he or she a frightening person or a benevolent figure? Do you remember sitting in your boss's office? Do you remember what it looked like? What your boss wore? How your boss addressed you and how you addressed your boss?

How did you feel on Mondays? How did you feel on Fridays? Were you dead tired at the end of the day? Mentally or physically? Or spiritually? Or did you often not want the day to end?

Did you look forward to retirement? Did they throw a party for you at work? Did they give you a gift? What was it? Was that embarrassing to you? Is there anyone still there whom you miss? Are you tempted to call or visit your office? Did you ever give in to the temptation?

Did you ever ride through rocky times at your workplace? Was your company sold or taken over?

Do you feel that you had a career, or a job? Would you call yourself ambitious? Did you ever run your own business? How did it start?

Was your profession a respected one in your community? Did you have a mentor? Were you a mentor? When did you realize that there was someone looking up to you as a professional person in your chosen career?

Did you wake up to an alarm, a clock radio, or the sun streaming through the window? What time did you get up? What time did you go to bed on a weeknight? Did you sleep late on the weekends? Did you ever work unusual hours? Graveyard or swing shift?

Were you ever fired or laid off? How did you cope with that? Did you ever have to go on unemployment? Were you promoted? Did it come unexpectedly, or did you let it be known you wanted the job? How did you feel and react when you heard the good news? Were you ever passed over for a position you thought you deserved? Who got it?

Do you remember your first kiss? What kind of dating did you do in high school? What is your favorite kind of date, even now? Who was your first love? Who broke whose heart?

Did you know, on the first day you met your spouse, that this would be your life's partner? How did you know? Did he or she know it, too? What did he say when he asked you to marry him? What did she answer? Where were you? Did he go talk to your father? How was it meeting his parents?

Describe your wedding. Your outfit. Your spouse's. Your mother's. Your father's. The bridal party. The church or hall. The reception. The food. Was there anything unusual in your wedding vows? Were your knees knocking? Who performed the ceremony?

What do you like best about your spouse? A physical attribute? A way of being or seeing? His laugh, perhaps? Or her smile? In your years of marriage, what have you learned about your spouse that you didn't know on your wedding day?

Can you name the china patterns, silver patterns, crystal patterns that you picked to be given to you as wedding gifts? What anniversary gift do you remember giving? What anniversary gift do you remember getting?

What song do you consider the most romantic? What term of endearment do you use for your spouse? What is your favorite picture of you two together? A wedding picture? An anniversary picture? What photo do you have that shows the true feelings between you two?

Describe your first apartment together. Your first house. Were they places you loved, or were they just making do?

Do you remember telling your husband that you were pregnant? Was it a surprise or a long-planned-for event? Do you remember telling your parents? What did your maternity clothes look like? Did you share with your friends? Did you suffer from morning sickness or have other problems?

Why did you name your children what you named them?

Which hospital did you deliver in? Do you remember the ride there? Do you remember the ride home? Did you send birth announcements when your babies were born? Did neighbors or relatives come to help out? Did you have a separate nursery all fixed up? How was it papered and painted? What did the crib look like? Did you hang a mobile over it?

What pet name did you use for your children when they were babies? Did you keep using them, even when the children grew older? What did your kids call you? The basic "Mommy" and "Daddy," or something more unusual? Did your babies have hair when they were born?

How did you decide which school to send your children to? Did they go to the neighborhood school, or did you send them to private or parochial school? Why? Were you involved in many carpools? Did you teach your child to drive?

Did your children play in the backyards in the neighborhood, or did you take them to a park?

Did you buy your children a set of encyclopedias? What kind? Where did you keep them? Did they use them very much?

Were you involved in the PTA or as a room parent at school? Did a teacher
ever call you in to discuss a problem or to tell you something about your child
that made you very proud?

Did your family attend a church or synagogue regularly? Did your children
attend religious school?

Who was your children's pediatrician? Did you ever have to take them to the emergency room?

Were the teenage years rugged for you and your children?

Can you remember one memorable thing that each of your children said,
something that surprised you or amused you or impressed you at the time and
still sticks in your mind?

How did you cope with taking your children to college?

What was the best trip you ever took with your children? What made it so good?

What was the address of the house you raised your family in? What was your phone number? Was your house a one-story, two-story? Stone, wood, or brick? Did you have a garage? A blacktop driveway? What was the floor plan? Did you use the back door as much as you used the front?

Why did you originally move to the town where you raised your family?
How did you pick the neighborhood? Did you choose it for the schools, for
the quiet, for the proximity to your workplace?

What kind of stove did you have? Gas or electric? Did you have linoleum on the kitchen floor? What was the pattern? What did your cookie jars and canisters look like? Where did you keep your onions and potatoes? Where did you throw your mail? Where did you keep your ironing board? Where did you do your wash?

What room did your family relax in together? Where did you go to get away from one another? Did the kids hang out in their rooms? What were the rules of the house? No phone calls after 10 P.M.? Last one in, lock the door? Where were your telephones?

Did you have a basement? What was down there? Did you have an attic?
What was up there? What was your favorite part of the house you raised
your family in? Why?

Did your family sit outside much in the summer? On a patio or a front stoop?
Did you have a screened-in porch? A front porch? Did you ever eat meals out
there?

When your children moved out, did the house feel like a different place? Did you like it as much?

Do you still live in that house? If not, how does it make you feel when you think of another family living there? Have you ever gone back to visit the house? Was it a good experience, or did you regret going?

What's your favorite candy bar? Where do you usually buy it? At the drugstore or the grocery store? How much does it cost now? How much did it cost when you were growing up? Was there a particular task you ever did that you would reward yourself for doing by buying yourself a candy?

What about ice cream? What kind do you like? Do you get it at an ice cream parlor, or in the freezer section of the store? Did your summers include walking to get ice cream cones? Who did you usually go with? Your brother or sister? Your best friend? Which is for you, sugar or cake cones?

What is your favorite perfume or cologne? Do you remember seeing an ad about it that intrigued you, or did you smell it on someone else and just have to have it? Did you ever receive your perfume as a surprise, or was it such a well-known fact about you that you got it for a present more often than not?

What's your favorite season? What do you like most/least about summer?
About fall? What special foods do you eat in the summer? How do you
winterize your home? Do you have flowers that bloom every spring?

Who is your sports team? Baseball? Basketball? Football? Pro? College? Would you say you are a superfan or a fair-weather friend? Have you ever met the coach? Do you respect him or her? Did you ever have a sports figure who was particularly meaningful to you? Did you ever get his or her autograph?

Do you have a favorite Broadway musical? Did you ever actually see it on stage, or do you just like the music? Who is your favorite artist? Do you identify with the artist's life in any way?

What is your favorite holiday? Where do you celebrate it? Where did you celebrate it when you were growing up?

Whose politics have you admired most? What President would you have
enjoyed voting for? Abraham Lincoln? Andrew Jackson? Who was the best
President of your lifetime?

Different times of life are satisfying for different reasons; which has been the most satisfying for you? Why? The three-kids-and-a-station-wagon stage? When you became the boss? When you were pursuing your higher education?

Who is your best friend? Why?

Do you have a favorite retreat or place of respite where you go to bring you silence and solace?

What is your favorite cartoon character or comic strip? Which comics do you remember reading when you were growing up?

What is your favorite restaurant? What special dish do you like to eat there? Do you know the maître d' or hostess? Are you friendly with the waiters and waitresses? Is there a toast you use time and time again?

What modern conveniences are your favorites? The portable phone? The remote control? As an "old dog," have you learned new tricks? Can you use a computer? Would you want to?

What is your favorite time of day? What was the best day of your life?

How do you like your eggs? Where do you usually get them, in a coffee shop or at home? Who makes them at your house? You or your spouse? What kind of omelette do you order?

What recipe are you famous for? For a small group? For a large group?
What dish do you usually bring to a potluck or picnic? What do you
remember as your mother's specialty item? Your grandmother's?

What would be your last supper? What is your favorite Campbell's soup?

Do you follow any rules of nutrition? Are you a vegetarian? Do you stay away from white sugar? Do you keep kosher? Eat fish on Friday? Avoid cholesterol?

Have you ever been on a diet? A faddish diet that "everyone" was on? What diet worked the best for you? How much do you remember losing?

What are your personal staples? What things do you keep around the house all the time?

What is your perfect breakfast? What is your usual breakfast? What is your perfect lunch? What is your usual lunch? What is your perfect dinner? What is your usual dinner?

What cookbook do you use the most? What one do you remember your mother using?

Are you allergic to any foods? Is there anything that you cannot and will not eat? Do you eat seafood? Have you ever eaten it at the shore?

Did you and your spouse often go dancing? Where? In a big dance pavilion?
Did you get excited when you pulled into the parking lot? Which dances did
you do? Where did you learn to do these dances?

When you and your friends got together socially as young adults, what did you do? Cards? Charades? Conversation? Small talk? Whose house did you go to most often, or did you trade off? What do you do when you get together now? How did you meet the friends you're most comfortable with?

Do you buy books new, or borrow them from the library? What is the last book you read? Why did you choose that one? Where were you sitting when you read it?

Are you friendly with your neighbors? Do you sit down together of an evening on the back porch or the patio? Or are you merely cordial with them, nodding acquaintances? Do you look out for one another's homes when one of you goes away? Have you ever had a neighbor whom you've loved and lost? Were you close with a family that later moved away?

Have you spent time doing charitable work? Did you put in legwork, hours on the phone, or office volunteer work? Are you a member of any charitable groups at your place of worship? Why was the good work you picked important to you? Did you meet people working there whom you would not have met in your everyday life?

Is there anything you need that you do not have?

Have you ever had surgery? Are you afraid of doctors?

Have you ever had to take legal action against anybody or had legal action
taken against you? Was it rough? How did you get along with your lawyer?
What was his or her office like?

Do you often go to galleries, the opera, or museums? Are you a patron of any cultural organizations? Why are you involved with the ones you've chosen? Did you ever have a desire to be an artist or a performer?

What magazines do you subscribe to? Which ones do you pick up at the drugstore or grocery? Do they tend to pile up on the floor beside your bed, or on the end table by your armchair? Are they the same magazines you've always read, or have they changed? Name a Life magazine cover you especially remember. A Time magazine cover. A Look magazine cover.

Who takes care of money in your house? Where do you keep your checkbook? Do you sit in the same spot every month to take care of your household business, or do you plop down at the kitchen table when the spirit moves you?

Do you and your spouse enjoy the same hobbies? Have you taken up any new ones together, or are your individual hobbies valuable time apart for you? Do you do most of the work around your house yourself, or do you hire people to do it? The housework, say, or the yardwork. Are you a putterer?

Has retirement been a positive or negative experience? Do you enjoy a slower pace now or find yourself as busy as ever?

Did you ever have to help one of your friends, or your spouse, through a family member's illness or death?

Do you believe in God or another higher power? Do you pray? Where do you go to worship?

Do you have a strong political party alliance? Have you ever worked on a campaign? Have you ever worked at a polling place? Where do you go to vote? Do you see the same people there every year? Which domestic problems are utmost in your town today? How have you noticed them firsthand?

Have you ever found yourself going against popular opinion or beliefs politically? Has this caused you any problems? Is there a government policy that you strongly disagree with? Do you think the welfare system is run correctly? Are your Social Security benefits what you think they should be?

How have you seen racial injustice firsthand? Have you ever been the
target of prejudice?

Has there been a case of corruption or scandal that has rocked your town?
Were you surprised when it came to light?

Have you ever been on jury duty? What was the case? Did you decide the defendant guilty or innocent? Was it a hard judgment call? Did it keep you awake at nights?

What have been your feelings about the space program? Where were you

when Neil Armstrong walked on the moon?

Do you own a flag? Do you display it? Do you feel the same way about politics and politicians as you did when you first became old enough to vote?

What do you think was America's grandest national moment during your lifetime? America's lowest national moment? What direction do you think the country is going in today? Are you optimistic or pessimistic about the nation's future?

How does being an American feel different from the way it felt forty years

ago?

How would you describe the community you live in now? Rural? Suburban? Urban? What about your state? Deep South? Midwest? Northeast? Are there mountains where you live? Lakes? A river? Beachfront? Did you ice-skate on the lake or canoe down the river?

What is the big business in the town you live in? What was the big business in the town you grew up in? Did you know any of the community leaders? Did you become one?

Are there major highways going through your town? What is the nearest airport? Have you spent much time there? How do people get to the airport in your town? Cab? Bus? Shuttle? Or is it close in enough that relatives and friends drop off and pick up one another?

What are your local newspapers? Has your name ever been mentioned in one? Has your picture ever appeared? Have you ever written a letter to the editor? Do you read them?

Do you use public transportation? Is it decent and fairly easy to use? Is it safe? How much does it cost? Where do you catch it? Where are you dropped off? What do you think about the drivers?

Have you ever had any dealings with the local police or firefighters? Have you had friends or relatives on the force? Which stations do you drive by regularly? What kind of action do you notice going on there?

Is there a local parade every year or an annual festival in your town? Are there any amusement parks or other tourist draws? Do you have a fair there? What time of the year does it happen? What foods do you eat at the fair?

Which buildings do you think about when you think about downtown? How would you describe the skyline? Have you seen it change over the years? What is the big department store where you live? Have most of the shoppers moved to malls? Indoor or outdoor malls? Do you go there often? What shops are there? Did you prefer shopping downtown?

Has any area of town been gentrified and changed very much since you've lived there? Do you remember the way it was before? Which do you prefer? What is the most popular steak house in town? The most popular seafood restaurant? Chinese restaurant? Pizza joint?

What are your local sports? Do you have a pro team? When out-of-towners think about your town, what do they think of? Your football team? Your famous clam chowder? Your supposedly crooked politicians? Skiing your mountains?

Do you have loved ones buried in the cemetery in town? Do you visit? Is it
maintained to your satisfaction?

Are you able to hear any public events—a football game, the fireworks—from the quiet of your backyard at night? What sounds do you hear in your neighborhood?

What is different about the home you live in now from the home you raised your family in? If you decided to move from the family home, what was the deciding factor? What do you like about where you live now? What do you dislike about it? Is there something about this home that you've always wanted in a home?

How did you feel each time you moved? Was it a hello or a good-bye?

What is the quirkiest aspect of your house? Enclosed stairs to the attic? A lavatory under the stairs? Do you have the bathroom you want? How would you change it? Do you have the kitchen you want? How would you change it?

Is your living room formal, or do you actually use it? What does your couch look like? Do you ever fall asleep on it? Do you keep a throw blanket on it to use when you're reading or watching TV? Which is the most comfortable room in your house? What do you spend time doing there?

Do you have any needlepoint sayings on a pillow or hanging on a wall? Do you have a favorite chair? Have you moved it from house to house with you? Where did you get it? When you bought it, did you sense that it would become your favorite?

Have you ever had a feud with your neighbors? How did you resolve it?

Do you spend much time in your bedroom, or do you go there only to sleep?
Do you watch TV in bed, read the newspaper in bed? Do you make your bed
every day? What do you see from your bedroom window? From your kitchen
window?

What time does your mail come? Is your mailbox right at your door, or do you have to walk a ways to get to it? Do you have your name on your mailbox? Where do you put your purse when you walk in the door? Where do you hang or place your keys? Do you lock your door day and night? Did you have to lock it thirty or forty years ago?

Do you park in your garage? Do you have a garage door opener? Is your garage organized or more of a messy storage space? What seasonal items do you keep there and haul out when the time comes?

Do you have the same table and chairs you had in the house where you raised your family? Have you had them refinished? Do you still sit at the same spot at the table as when you were raising your children?

What would your dream house be?

Have you experienced a natural disaster? An earthquake? A flood? How was your family affected?

What grocery store do you use? Which is the first aisle you go down? How much does a usual trip to the store cost you? Do you use coupons? Do you buy in bulk? What grocery stores did you used to go to? Which was your favorite? Why?

What drugstore do you go to? Do you know the pharmacist by name? What else do you chat about, other than your prescriptions?

If you have been slowed by age, which simple activities do you miss?

What part of housework do you hate the most? How was it always split up in your family? Did the men generally do the outside work while the women took care of the inside? Did you ever have household help? Was that hard for you to get used to?

✍

What type of store do you like to browse in? Bookstores? Hardware stores? Cookware stores? Garden stores? Or do you hate shopping altogether?

What's your daily routine? Do you get up, drink coffee, have a shower? Drink tea, go get the paper? Watch a morning television show, listen to a certain radio program, call a certain friend?

What route do you take around your house at night before you finally turn in? Do you lock the door, chain it, set the timer on the coffeepot, turn on the light in the hall, brush your teeth, set the alarm? Are you ever too tired to do these things, or would you be unable to fall asleep if you didn't?

How do you spend your time outdoors? Walking? Just sitting and enjoying the air? Gardening? Flower or vegetable? What do you grow?

Do you keep your old photos in an album or a shoebox? How often do you take them out and look at them? Who took most of the pictures?

What beauty parlor or barber shop do you go to? What is your beautician or barber's name? Do you have a standing appointment? How often do you go there? What do you usually have done? A perm, color, a cut? A shave or just a haircut? Do you ever get your nails done? What magazines do they have there for customers to read?

What is your doctor's name? Your dentist? Have you gone to the same person for a while, or have you recently switched? If you have, why?

Are you usually late or early? Do you like to be alone? What do you do on rainy days? Would you say you're lucky?

Are you more comfortable speaking, or writing? Do you enjoy talking on the phone more than writing letters? How much did postage stamps cost when you began to be aware of such things?

Do you play the lottery? Have you ever won? Where do you buy your tickets? Which games do you play?

Do you like music in the house, or silence? Do you turn on the TV for company? Do you doodle? What figures tend to come up? Boxes? Circles? Faces?

Have you ever smoked cigarettes? What brand? What was their slogan? What did the package look like? How much did they cost? How much do they cost now? Where do you buy them? Do you wish you didn't smoke? Do you have a habit you'd like to break? How about one you'd like to start?

Are you a list maker? List your responsibilities.

What was the first funeral you attended? How did it affect you? What was the last one you went to? Are they getting easier or harder?

Is your calendar messy or neat? Where do you hang your calendar? On the back of your broom closet door? Do you keep a desk or pocket calendar? Do you buy the same kind every year? Do you use a dictionary often? Do you keep it by your chair, or up on the bookshelf?

When someone sneezes, do you say "Gesundheit" or "God bless you"? Do you have other sayings that just naturally come out of your mouth?

Do you read the Bible or a daily meditation book? Where do you keep it?
Beside your bed? Did somebody special give it to you? Did somebody special
teach you about its importance?

Describe what you look like now. Have you been happy with the way you look? What did you look like as a teenager? As a young child? Do you have any birthmarks or scars that differentiate your looks absolutely from anyone else you know? Who do you look like most in your family? Is there a family look, would you say, making your kin recognizable all the way down the line? Do your children look like you, or like your spouse?

Do you remember getting your first suit and tie? Your first nylons and heels? Do you prefer big purses or small pocketbooks? What fashion trends have you seen come and go? Pantsuits, middie blouses, stretch pants, leisure suits? Did you own any of these? Did you follow the trends? Was one of them right for you—particularly flattering?

What jewelry do you wear? A wedding band? A pin of your mother's? A watch of your father's? A charm bracelet? Where did you get the charms? Do you wear anything that represents your children or grandchildren? Have you ever worn hats? What kind of shoes are you partial to?

Who called you from the hospital to tell you your first grandchild was born? What time was it? Who was the first person you called? Were you able to go see the new family in the hospital? Did you take a gift? What did you think the first minute the nurse brought the baby to the room?

Were you able to go over to the house much and help out with the new baby?
Did you cook dinner for the new family or bathe the baby? Did you stay
over, or come and go in the mornings and evenings?

When did your grandchild first say your name? Were you at your house or at the child's house? What do your grandchildren call you? Did you ever make anything by hand for your grandchild? A sweater? A wooden toy? A quilt? Did you enjoy shopping for the baby? What clothes did you buy? What toys did you buy?

Did you baby-sit often? At their house? At your house? Do you have a special room for the grandchildren at your house? What toys do you keep there? Do your grandchildren ever come spend the night with you? How do you spend those evenings? Have you taught your grandchildren any games or hobbies? Do you play cards with them? Have you taught them cooking or baking or fishing? What television shows do you and your grandchildren watch together?

Have you ever taken your grandchildren on a trip with you? One at a time,
or in a group? Were you satisfied with the way these trips turned out? Have
you gone to the movies together? A play? A circus?

What souvenirs did you bring your grandchildren from your travels? Do any of your grandchildren have a collection that you keep adding to?

What do you fix your grandchildren to eat when they come to visit you?

Can you see your face anywhere in your grandchild's face? What one thing would you like to be sure your grandchildren remember? What do you want them to remember about you?

Where do you like to go on vacation? Is there a certain time of year when you always take your trips? Is there any place you've been that you'd really like to visit again? Which restaurant do you hope is still there? Would you try to stay at the same hotel? What was it about that place that would draw you again—the physical beauty of the surroundings or a happy memory of a personal time?

Which airport do you find yourself in most when traveling? How has it changed over the years? Is it full of shops and foodstands? Is there something you like to get or see there every time you pass through? What is the key to getting along on a trip? Have you always been glad to get home?

What are you driving now? How many years have you had your car? When did you get your first car? Did you buy it for yourself, or did your parents help you? How much did you pay? How much did a tank of gas cost in those days? Where did you usually fill up? Who taught you to drive? What was that like? Were you intimidated? Did you learn on a stick shift?

Have you had a recurring dream throughout your life? What do you think it means?

What makes you angry? How do you handle being deeply upset? What are you like when you're sick? Do you like to be taken care of or left alone? Are you a dreamer or a realist?

Is there someone you talk with every day? Your sister? Your daughter? A best friend or neighbor? Do you have someone you confide in, or do you keep your troubles to yourself? Who comes to you with their troubles? How do you think you help them?

*Did you have definite goals? Did you achieve them? Are you still working on
them? Any new ones?*

If you hold a fundamental truth, what is it?

Are there any other memories you would like to write about?

ONE MORE QUESTION

WE'D LIKE to ask you yet another question. We're wondering if you would like to share the family history you have preserved—share it with generations to come.

If you've answered the questions in *To Our Children's Children Journal of Family Memories*, you know that stories beget stories, that one memory leads to another, allowing moments of life to be rekindled in your mind.

Just as the stories of your family prime the well of your own memory, they can help others tell their stories. Hearing other people's stories reminds us of happenings in our own lives. Before we know it we are traveling all the marvelous tangents of memory that lead us off from there.

If you have a favorite answer to one of the questions in this journal, we'd love for you to share it with us. If you'd like to choose a story or two that you enjoyed telling while preserving your family history, we will try to gather a collection for a future volume. Your stories will help others pass along their own.

You can mail a copy of your story to:

> To Our Children's Children
> P.O. Box 1086
> Virginia City, Nevada 89440

Thanks. We look forward to hearing from you.

About the Authors

BOB GREENE is a syndicated columnist for the *Chicago Tribune*. His column appears in more than two hundred newspapers in the United States, Canada and Japan, and may be read daily at www.chicago.tribune.com/go/greene/. For nine years his "American Beat" was the lead column in *Esquire* magazine; as a broadcast journalist he has served as contributing correspondent for *ABC News Nightline*. In addition to *To Our Children's Children*, his national bestsellers include *Hang Time: Days and Dreams with Michael Jordon*; *Be True to Your School*; and *Good Morning, Merry Sunshine*.

D. G. FULFORD is a freelance journalist and award-winning former columnist for the *Los Angeles Daily News* and the *New York Times* News Service.

Greene and Fulford are brother and sister.